An Oration

Also from Westphalia Press
westphaliapress.org

The Idea of the Digital University

Masonic Tombstones and Masonic Secrets

Eight Decades in Syria

Avant-Garde Politician

L'Enfant and the Freemasons

Baronial Bedrooms

Conflicts in Health Policy

Material History and Ritual Objects

Paddle Your Own Canoe

Opportunity and Horatio Alger

Careers in the Face of Challenge

Bookplates of the Kings

Collecting American Presidential Autographs

Misunderstood Children

Original Cables from the Pearl Harbor Attack

Social Satire and the Modern Novel

The Amenities of Book Collecting

The Genius of Freemasonry

A Definitive Commentary on Bookplates

James Martineau and Rebuilding Theology

No Bird Lacks Feathers

Earthworms, Horses, and Living Things

The Man Who Killed President Garfield

Anti-Masonry and the Murder of Morgan

Understanding Art

Homeopathy

Ancient Masonic Mysteries

Collecting Old Books

The Boy Chums Cruising in Florida Waters

The Thomas Starr King Dispute

Ivanhoe Masonic Quartettes

Lariats and Lassos

Mr. Garfield of Ohio

The Wisdom of Thomas Starr King

The French Foreign Legion

War in Syria

Naturism Comes to the United States

New Sources on Women and Freemasonry

Designing, Adapting, Strategizing in Online Education

Gunboat and Gun-runner

Meeting Minutes of Naval Lodge No. 4 F.A.A.M

An Oration
Delivered Before the
Municipal Authorities of the City of Boston
at the Celebration of the
Seventy-Sixth Anniversary
of the Declaration of
American Independence, July 5, 1852

by Thomas Starr King, A.M.

WESTPHALIA PRESS
An imprint of Policy Studies Organization

An Oration: Delivered Before the Municipal Authority of the City of Boston
All Rights Reserved © 2014 by Policy Studies Organization

Westphalia Press
An imprint of Policy Studies Organization
1527 New Hampshire Ave., NW
Washington, D.C. 20036
info@ipsonet.org

ISBN-13: 978-1-63391-080-5
ISBN-10: 1633910806

Cover design by Taillefer Long at Illuminated Stories:
www.illuminatedstories.com

Daniel Gutierrez-Sandoval, Executive Director
PSO and Westphalia Press

Rahima Schwenkbeck, Director of Media and Marketing
PSO and Westphalia Press

Updated material and comments on this edition
can be found at the Westphalia Press website:
www.westphaliapress.org

The Organization of Liberty on the Western Continent.

AN

ORATION

DELIVERED BEFORE THE

MUNICIPAL AUTHORITIES

OF THE

CITY OF BOSTON,

AT THE

CELEBRATION OF THE SEVENTY-SIXTH ANNIVERSARY

OF THE

Declaration of American Independence,

JULY 5, 1852.

BY THOMAS STARR KING, A.M.

BOSTON:
ROCKWELL AND CHURCHILL, CITY PRINTERS.
1892.

CITY OF BOSTON.

IN BOARD OF ALDERMEN, December 21, 1891.

WHEREAS, The Fourth of July Oration delivered in 1852 by Rev. THOMAS STARR KING is the only one of the series since 1822 which has not been printed; and as his family is willing that it should now be issued,

ORDERED, That the Chairman of the Record Commissioners, under the direction of the Committee on Printing, cause the said Oration to be printed, bound, and distributed; the edition to consist of fifteen hundred copies: and the expense, not to exceed four hundred dollars, to be charged to the appropriation for Printing.

Passed. Sent down for concurrence. December 23 came up concurred.

Approved by the Mayor December 26, 1891.

A true copy.

Attest:

JOHN T. PRIEST, *Asst. City Clerk.*

PREFACE.

THOMAS STARR KING was born in the city of New York, Dec. 17, 1824, his father being the Rev. Thomas F. King, and his mother Susan Starr, both natives of that city. His father became the pastor of a church in Charlestown, where he died before his son was qualified to enter college. The young man however continued his studies while serving as a public school teacher and clerk in the Navy Yard, and in September 1846 he succeeded Rev. E. H. Chapin in the pulpit which his father had occupied. In December 1848 he married Miss Julia M. Wiggin, and soon after was installed at Hollis-street church, Boston, where he continued for eleven years. His popularity as a preacher and lecturer was very great, and few men have gained more devoted or appreciative friends.

"It was," says Dr. Henry W. Bellows, "the hidden, interior man of the heart, the invisible character behind all the rich possessions, intellectual and social, of this gifted man, that gave him his real power and skill to control the wills, and to move the hearts, and to win the unbounded confidence and affection of his fellow-beings."

In 1860, Mr. King accepted a call from a church in San Francisco. His fame as a lecturer as well as a preacher had preceded him, and he was called upon to visit all parts of our western coast. At the outbreak of the Rebellion he was thus in a position to exert a great influence upon the public of California, then tempted by the suggestion of a Pacific republic. No one who reads the pages of this oration can doubt the energy or the eloquence with which Mr. King combatted this heresy, nor the unflinching support which he gave to the cause of the Union. "He went forth appealing to the people taking the constitution and Washington for his text," and he is confessedly entitled to the credit of having preserved the Pacific states to the Union.

In January 1864 his new church edifice was dedicated, but after a brief illness with diphtheria he died March 4, 1864.

Mr. King published in 1859 a well-known book in regard to the White Hills, whose beauties were his favorite theme, and which, in a popular sense, he almost discovered. Several volumes of his sermons were printed after his death; but during his life-time his compositions were reserved for use on the lecture-platform. It was owing to this fact, that the following Oration was not published as usual, at the date of its delivery, by the City of Boston. Finding recently that this was the only one in the series of Fourth of July Orations, delivered by request of the City of Boston, which had not been printed, application was made to the widow and children of Mr. King, and their consent was readily given to the publication. The manuscript was found to be in perfect form, and only one or two verbal corrections have been needed.

W. H. W.

CITY HALL, BOSTON, March 4, 1892.

THE ORGANIZATION OF LIBERTY ON THE WESTERN CONTINENT.

Mr. Mayor and Fellow-citizens:

The seventy-sixth anniversary of the day which proclaimed our country a distinct and independent power on the earth has dawned upon us. And it finds us in such prosperity and peace, and such rapidly increasing greatness, that our thoughts are invited to rise in adoration and gratitude to Him who "hath not dealt so with any nation," and whose favor alone is permanent strength.

The topic to which I shall ask your attention is the "Organization of Liberty on the Western Continent." In connection with this theme the Fourth of July at once assumes its real importance in our whole history, and unveils its highest claim to our reverent memory and lasting gratitude.

The day is distinguished by its historical marriage with the Declaration of Independence; but it is not the production of that vigorous revolutionary rhetoric that we celebrate. Literature abounds with denunciations of oppressions and assertions of human worth and rights, that have higher quality than the periods of our venerated state paper, and yet we do not dignify them with national holidays. We venerate the Declaration as *a deed* more than as a composition or a collection of doctrines. It was a bold blow for the liberty of three millions of people; and we should honor the noble manner in which the deed was done, — the deliberate and solid statesmanship that comprehended the responsibilities, and took upon its shoulders the duties of such a radical position, — more than the words and the deed together.

In fact, the whole Revolution itself is not of any great importance in military history as a series of battles and a protest of physical force. Its achievements in the field are immortalized by the cause it served and the manner of the service. Our revolution was turned into a dignified force instead of a flash of enthusiasm and a rattle of musketry, by the compact, passive resistance of character and the moral fidelity to the cause, in privation and suffering, manifested all over the land; through these qualities it stood in right relations with the gravity of our earlier history, and offered no obstructions, but powerful aid rather, to the completion of the destiny to which from the first our land was pledged — *the peaceful organization of Liberty.*

Let us glance for a moment at the physical universe, and catch a few of the broad instructions given in it, as to the relative value of the process of organization. Nature is not satisfied with a boundless treasury of elements and a happy balance of them into inorganic harmonies. She sends up a chorus of praise to God as the organizer as well as creator; for her materials are combined into forms, and the spirit that superintends our world revels in varieties of form that defy numeration.

The globe we live on is thoroughly organized by an array of antagonistic forces, and is made to play as a wheel of a celestial orrery. The clouds, the tides, the winds, are wrapped by laws, and made through their movement and their oscillations to manifest subtle harmonies that cannot be broken. Yea, even the light is made to obey a steady rein, and to be punctual as time, and exact as mathematics, in the dispensation of its floods. The dancing light is not suffered to be capricious and fitful in its visitations, but is required to be dutiful, and so that it shall break here and there in flashes, or stream in vivid sheets now and then athwart the darkness. Nature builds a huge home for it, stretches the immense diameter and bends the solid arches of the sun, whose gravitation poises a colony of planets, and around that rocky orb she winds the vesture of flame that is to light and warm the globes that reach from Mercury to Neptune. The steps of the vast annals of nature are marked by rising grades of organization. Each new stratum is deposited as the condition and abode of a higher animated structure; and at last the supreme skill embodied in the frame of man announces that the periods of geological development are passed.

And in history the great work is that of social organization. Providence designs that there shall be not only myriads of persons on his globe, but also civil and social structures, by which individuals shall be disposed in right relations, and many members become one body. The organization of justice, therefore, is the task which is proposed to the human race. It has steadily struggled up through the centuries towards the attainment of it; and the cheering epochs of history are those when greater advances are made and new successes permanently gained.

The student delights to retreat by his sympathies into such luminous seasons of the past as when the Greek intellect was busy in the organization of beauty in statues, temples, eloquence, and verse; or the Egyptian genius was throwing up from the sombre depths of its sense of the Infinite, the Sphinx, the pyramids, and the wild literature of future judgment and transmigration; or when the sinews of Roman valor and statesmanship were opening paths to the possession of the world; or when Italy was feeding the eyes of Europe with the rapid wonders of her chisel and the magic of her brush: but though less fascinating to poetic sensibilities, those are the most eminent most grand and most powerful epochs of civilization when some great institutions loom up shaped by the skill of many hands, beneficient in their purpose and their agency, standing on the firm basis of right and supporting themselves by their own symmetry.

We shall be confirmed in this view of history from whatever quarter we study it. Regarding it as philosophers and watching for the advance of truth, we shall see that no triumph of truth is so important and so enduring as when it domesticates itself in strong institutions and becomes entrenched in the habits of race. Regarding it religiously, and anxious for the victory of right, we must see that there is no conquest so valuable as when justice descends into the practical life of an age, and builds its massive defences around men, investing them with rights which by general consent are considered sacred as their personality. Or if we look at history as philanthropists, still the most important and gratifying seasons will seem to be those when the welfare of men is something more than a matter of sentiment and sympathy, but is protected by the might of law and hedged by generous statutes.

The man who, by the more quiet methods of personal influence, organizes in the world a dumb institution, does vastly more than he whose radical eloquence sets the deformities of society and life in the blaze of an angry idea. The foundation of a charity school is a more memorable event than the most eloquent invective that could be preached against the selfish use of riches; a new Christian character in which religious truth is freshly embodied is a more precious contribution to the world than a new theory of holiness. History does not take account of all the hazy theories that stain the night air of time with transient radiance, any more than the charts of Astronomy make account of the Boreal flashes and the meteors that adorn the winter nights with their fitful and fantastic fire. It is only when a theory or an intellectual movement, ceasing to be a superficial phenomenon, becomes a vital power, — a subject not for cool geometrical measurements, but a dynamic energy — and spreading through the intellect of genius and the sympathies of the people, (as in the case of the principles uttered in the Reformation, and by the first Wesleyan preachers), manifests itself as a constructive force and adds new institutions to the social landscape, which are vital from the core, that it marks another hour in the advance of the race.

How easy is it to start *à priori*, and reasoning down from some exalted abstract principles to condemn and scout the injustice that is woven in with society, or by putting together a few ideas to sketch out a perfect plan of state, and home, and church. It is pastime for our reveries. But to make our criticisms available; to give our dreams a fulcrum by which they can start rooted disorders; to make our reveries practical and congruous with facts of human nature, and laws of the world: we had better try that work before we set up claims to wisdom. There is no more marvellous manifestation of human superiority than the ability to put an advance political notion in practice, so that the machine will play easily and obey the calculated laws. What an expenditure of perfect philosophies before a new and higher *fact* is born! Humanity burns up tons of books to get light enough for one step ahead.

Alas! gentlemen, it is not the mere existence of steam, either in the social or the physical world, that works wonders for humanity. It is very easy to have steam. A little water, a match, some charcoal, and a tea-kettle, supply all the conditions for raising it, so that an enthusiast may descant at leisure upon its properties, and enjoy its prophetic and eloquent hiss. But before the steam era in the world history begins, *the engine* must appear out of the resources of some practical organizing brain, and offer its sinewy and complicated body for that intense, vapory soul.

In the light of this analogy we say that the peculiarity of our own history is the steady and peaceful process of organization which it reveals, and by which higher political truth, which the world considered dangerous, was vindicated as practical by being slowly clothed in fact.

Other nations have looked back to a dim antiquity for their origin. The story of their growth has been that of struggle through barbarisms and superstitions, and against wrongs and errors that were entrenched behind centuries of prescription and habit. The changes for the better have been slow, and have cost immense effort and sacrifice. Principles have dawned and then darkened, perhaps drowned, as they rise, in the red mist of war. Explosions have scattered and wasted the beneficent forces of progress; lapses of popular virtue have sunk the hopes that were justified by rising truth; and the general picture given to us is that of a feeble germ of order, striving slowly against a chaotic mass of passion, prejudice, ignorance, and wrong, by which it is often defeated, and into which up to the present time it has succeeded in throwing but few of its threads of regulated liberty.

Until the Saxon colonization of this continent, such was the stereotyped form of national experience. But with the new theatre of action prepared by Providence, a new work was imposed. There was a slow process of discovering great principles, after the foundations of our society were laid, and then a fierce contest for their first existence on our soil. The old forces and conditions of progress with which Europe had been acquainted, — strife of class against class for new power or old privilege, civil war, compromise, foreign pressure, and the shifting attitudes of diplomacy, — have had no appreciable, certainly no important, effect upon our progress; it has been a rapid development of a few vigorous convictions and principles into form. It has been growth like that of an oak from its seed, by gradual absorption of heat, air, and moisture, with the occasional assistance of a storm. We are accustomed to speak of our great struggle as the War of *Revolution*, but strictly speaking it was the War of *Separation* only; for it did not bring any new organic principle into the field of our politics, but was a resistance to the obstructions that cramped the swelling energies of our fundamental convictions. No one of our constructive ideas has ever been quickened by the angry sacrifice of blood drawn by intestine war.

The last two centuries have been the most remarkable of the world's history for the amount of social justice that has been established for millions of men; and the fullest experience of it has been on this continent, secured by the institutions which have made our country an original experiment and spectacle in the annals of time. To a scientific mind, a Humboldt or an Owen, no tidings would be freighted with such absorbing interest as the information that a new and high type of organization had arisen on this planet; that the creative powers around us had given birth to some beautiful planet, some majestic tree, some strange and symmetrical animal, with higher functions and more intricate constitution than any vegetable or physical organization known to the lists of science. With what reverence would their minds bend before such a glorious miracle; and how eager, how curious and minute, would their researches be into the wisdom embodied in this last and highest creation of the intellect that rules the world!

We all know what excitement was caused, a few years since, by the discovery of a new planet beyond the path of Uranus. But what would the amazement of an astronomer be if he could detect in the sky a planet in the swift process of formation? Or what if he could look through his glass into some sacred district of space and see a vast continent of chaos organize itself rapidly into an orderly system; if every process by which planets and satellites are formed out of primeval matter, could be made visible, and the forces which upon our globe have so slowly deposited the landmarks of geological ages should condense their work into a few years, so that he could study it at leisure, night by night, noting each week some stage of advance which on our globe exhausted a thousand centuries, and seeing all ending in the production of a beauty which our globe and our system do not wear? What privilege would be accounted equal to this by an earnest, scientific mind, and how much more clearly would the study of such a creative process of nature reveal what the physical forces are, than any abstract description could convey; and how much deeper and more solemn the impression of such a spectacle than dry statements, chemical hypotheses and mathematical formulas!

And so our history is most interesting and suggestive when viewed as a fresh creation from the deeps of human nature that had long been sluggish, and whose vitality seemed to be effete. The appearance of our mighty millions of white democracy, stretched from ocean to ocean and from the Russian latitudes to the Tropical Gulf, without a monarch, with no hereditary rulers, no lords, no titles, no vested rights, no despotic

Church, but blest with an order such as the world has never seen, and a prosperity that has outrun every enthusiastic dream, and yet not exhausting more than half a century in the revelation of most startling results, — what is it to the political student but a process parallel to the picture we imagined, of an evolving system of worlds in space before the eye of an astronomer, a magnificent and astonishing effort of organization, unexampled in human experience for the breadth of the scale, the rapidity of the development, and the character of the products, and revealing as nothing else has ever done or could do, the constructive powers that slumber in the popular brain and heart.

Many of the facts of our history in which the Old World was concerned, catch a providential hue, when seen, from the principle that this continent was wanted for new organizations of society. We see a pregnant coincidence in the fact that the colonization did not begin till after the Protestant reformation had established itself, and that the Spaniards found no motives to claim and people the northern seaboard. A light is thrown upon the strenuous struggle of England and France in relation to a portion of our territory; the great expenditure of blood and treasure; and the skilful diplomacy which drove the French from the valley of the Ohio, — thus preparing the way for the consolidation of the American colonies, — giving them a friend in the government of France, while it banished from the great Western domains a race too much incumbered with the traditions of the past and too feeble in the faculties of organization to be worthy or able to dot that fresh country with new forms of government and society. Especially we are called to study reverently the process by which the Protestant world was first sifted and winnowed, till the choicest germs of character were found strong enough to send out the shoots of lasting institutions on a hard soil and under a hostile sky.

Nothing strikes the student with more force, as he looks back over the rise of our republic, than the small proportion of published or meditated theorizing about the rights of man, the province of government, and the destiny of our race, compared with the actual results that are visible. We have already intimated that there are two great classes of men related to the world's progress. One class are fine critics of social disorder and injustice in the light of favorite ideas. They are accurate analysts; perhaps they are able to make outlines and draughts of a polity or society that would exclude most of the evils that oppress mankind; but they have no force in the world. They cannot interest men in their plans, and the moment they come in contact with the real forces of society and human nature they and their theories are powerless as babes. All their energy runs to the brain and expends itself through the voice and the proportions of a theory.

If the world were made of paper, if ink were the life-blood of the universe, and things were no deeper than a mathematician's diagram, they would be the hope and salvation of the race. But the world is made up of something quite different from paper; and so we may rejoice that there is another class of men who have far less skill in theories, but far greater constructive capacity in the world of facts, men of influence, men who, wherever you place them, become centres of force, and soon dispose men and circumstances into an order where they move with more harmony and efficiency. Compared with the class first named, these last are as the seed of a tree in contrast with a clear description of it, or the chemical formulas of what its substance is. To use a sentence of Carlyle, "there is in them what transcends all logic utterance, a congruity with the unuttered." They live, and, "institutions are their lengthened shadows." Need I say that the men who first colonized the Plymouth sands and the shores of Boston bay were of the latter stamp. They had not spent much time in reveries about liberty as an ideal goddess. They came to labor as soon as they stepped upon the soil, with the undertone of conviction that freedom, as a working power, — a Hercules rather than an Apollo, a hero of toil, more than a patron of theories and dreams, — was to use them as the first channels through which its creative energy could pour itself into new forms for the benefit of many generations.

The men who stepped upon the bleak shores of New England had been so trained by hardship and oppression that every free sentiment their breasts harbored was as stubborn as their ribs, and every idea of rights which their heads supported had roots that were twisted in the sub-soil of their being. The strength of their faith in liberty could not be expressed in declamation or treatise; wherever they lived the effluence of their characters would have purified the social air, and their daily work have assisted the establishment of social righteousness.

Let us imagine an intelligent man, wholly ignorant of our earliest annals, but aware that the institutions and power of this country are the products of the last two centuries, beginning an examination of the primitive records of the New England settlements. Would he not expect to find some clearly outlined scheme of a great State and a Briarean government? Would he not confidently search for the sketch of a civil constitution and a theory of political equality and balances which the colonists determined that the forests should make way for, and the wise labor of their posterity strengthen and extend? How surprised would he be to discover that there were no such schemes; that the vessels that discharged the colonists were disburthened of no such theories! Or rather, the theories were *in the blood* of the men themselves.

What they sought and determined to gain was a few fundamental rights that would hedge their manhood and their faith. They wanted a simple, social structure, humble as their log-huts and Puritan chapels, that would house a prosperous and pious community and a peaceful brotherhood. They were not furious for the aggressive establishment of a social philosophy; their vitality had not been expended brain-wards in shaping and perfecting the ideal proportions of a pet theory. They had no more decided the minutiæ of their policy than they had decided on what spot they would put their dwellings; and so they had the immense advantage of grappling directly with circumstances by the working passions of men and the strong forces of their common sense, from which, in its purification by suffering, the crusts of feudal prejudice had dropped.

How much better for humanity that a Carver, a Winthrop, or a Brewster, were landed here with their circles of friends, than that the partisans of some Plato's "Republic," or Harrington's "Oceana," or Owen's "Harmony," had been disembarked! Each one of the men who were sent by Providence was a vitalized treatise, a seed corn of better societies and new ages. They came to build the institutions of the future, not by copying from any comprehensive, sharp-lined, radical vision, but by discharging into their first work a flood of rough vitality that could not but swell beyond its rind and gather larger structures for its home. They labored for the future and undreamed America as the beavers understand masonry and statics; and like the bees, the tiny Paxtons of entomology, whose geometry is not learned from Euclid but pervades their substance.

They had, too, the balance of powers that is necessary to every vigorous and lasting structure of society. They were bold, very bold, but not too bold. No set of men, however logical their protests against false habits and base laws, however clear their perceptions of truthful principles, can put much vital force into a new constructive movement if they are not consecrated and loyal men; if, in the centre of their being, they do not account themselves as subjects and instruments, and look toward some quarter of the Infinite with the shaded gaze of worship. In our ancestors, their faith, their courage, and the licentious iconoclasm to which the fresh forests might have invited their sense of wrong, were steadied and corrected by their reverence. They were not so out of patience with the past and with the land that had wronged them, that they could not appreciate its real wisdom, and be content to use what had worked well in their own country's experience. Repelled by the bitter experience of persecution from many of the ideas and social principles which were inwoven with the structure of society in the Old World, their minds swung with the centrifugal force of a planet towards a new order; and yet were bolted, by an energy firm and still as the centripetal rein, to a regular track.

It is fortunate that they did not come here with any schemes based on a dissection of human nature, and strive to anticipate centuries, if not to wrestle against the truth, by building a social fabric on the results of a shadowy analysis. They had not, like Fourier and his disciples, made any scientific inventory of the possible constructive powers of our nature, which they were eager to reflect in a community. If they had, the aboriginal communities in the American forests of wild cats, partridges and raccoons, would have received little detriment from a spreading civilization.

Instead of such an aim they affirmed the responsibilities of authorities. They had constructed no schemes of " hypominor " groups and " hyperminor " series in a perfect society, nor of " passional dominants " and " passional tonics," nor of the low accords and the cardinal accords of friendship, nor of the relative rank of ambition, love, and " familism " as forces in the state; but they struck for the intervention of the people in public affairs. They had not speculated finally about the precise ties that should connect the individual and the state, but they looked out for personal liberty, and they guaranteed trial by jury. The scheme of a phalanstery, in which children should be swung in a community of cradles, and trained from their "initial crisis" to their "citerior transition," (that is, from the moment when the baby gown is wanted to the time when the jacket shows symptoms of development), had never entered their heads; but they knew how to make the home sacred with the spirit of piety, and to startle nature with the humble architecture of the public school. No visions of landscapes laid out in geometrical order and proportioned nicely to the tastes of the cultivators had woven themselves out of the gossamer tissue into which truth may be unravelled by a diseased analysis, but they provided that roads should be built, and that land should not be prevented from partition by laws of primogeniture. They could not have conceived such finespun harmonies of structure in an ideal state as Plato outlined and St. Simon meditated, but they knew how to fix the running gear of a social order that should give a larger degree of homely justice than the world had imagined possible; they knew how to give beneficent power to grand juries, constables, and judges; how to appoint registrars, clerks, and surveyors;

how to hedge the town-meeting with solemn forms, and to keep a determined eye on the *Habeas Corpus*. Coming out of ages of feudalism and despotism, they had the sturdy sense "to ordain the maximum of administration and the minimum of government," "to keep power as much as possible in the hands of those most disposed to suffer from its abuses;" and to place the conservative element, (as Mr. Hillard has so wisely and so happily said,) "not in the limitation of political rights, but in the multiplication of political trusts."

The founders of our land organized the American township, the grandest practical movement of the human intellect hitherto made in society, since it reversed the old methods by which political existence and civil rights had been slowly communicated from the superior classes downward, and affirmed them for the whole people, and guarded each man's possession of them by the magic ring of law. This was the archetypal leaf which contained the secret of the structure of the plant, the primitive cell which throughout nature is the nucleus from which the highest organisms start, and by the multiplication of which they are easily formed. So great was the genius shown in the structure of these townships, and so vast and far-reaching their importance, that De Tocqueville's eulogy is justified, — "The boldest theories of the human reason were put into practice by a community so humble that no statesman condescended to attend to it; and a legislation without precedent was produced off-hand by the imagination of the citizens."

From the township the county was developed, and gradually the lineaments of an organized colony began to show themselves through the practical application of the idea of representative government, which another French writer of our century has called "one of the few great discoveries that among the moderns has created a new universe." From the earliest times and in every colony there seems to have been something in the air and soil of America to foster the idea of representative power as a first principle of American thought. We should all be acquainted with the quaint phrases in which an old historian informs us concerning Virginia, that, "In 1620 a house of burgesses broke out in the Colony." Such an eruption shows us what was the quality of the popular blood. What does it teach us but that the flushes of indignation at threatened oppression in the first settlements were not destructive but creative movements, opening legal and orderly channels for their vent? What was this strange eruption but the blush of American expression upon the infant countenance of the body politic, which was to be confirmed and stamped into it as a characteristic in coming years? The same historian writes, too, that in Massachusetts, "although there is no color for it in the Charter, a House of Deputies suddenly appeared in 1634, to the surprise of the Magistrates and the disappointment of their scheme for power." Whence could such a beneficient apparition have started but from the deeps of the American passion for freedom, which has proved itself wiser than all the schemes of studious critics of liberty, and which thus far has known how to meet every emergency from the resources of its organizing common sense?

There is something quite amusing in the tone with which Massachusetts met the proposition of friendly Lords in England to grant them and their families hereditary honors, if they should remove to this land. The proposition was not met by any clear argument against the injustice of it, or its discordance with their plans of society; it was rebutted by an odd expression of reverence which showed more convincingly than the most forcible logic could, how hopeless was the prospect of transplanting such honors into American respect; — "When God blesseth any branch of any noble or generous family with a spirit and gifts fit for government, it would be a taking of God's name in vain to put such a talent under a bushel, and a sin against the honor of magistracy to neglect such in our public elections. But if God should not delight to furnish some of their posterity with gifts fit for magistracy, we should expose them and the Commonwealth to reproach and prejudice, if we should call them forth, when God doeth not, to public authority." A fresh, cool blast of political truth setting back upon the sickly air of Europe from the pious democracy of the wilderness!

Various as were the forms of colonial constitution in America, and however contrary the claim might be to the letter and spirit of the charters, representative government was insisted on as a fundamental necessity, indispensable to the control of their own interests and the security of future freedom. Struck to the earth by the oppressions of the Old World, the Saxon Antæus rose up from contact with the aboriginal soil, surcharged with this instinct of representative rights, which was yet to prove fatal to his foe.

Rhode Island attained and kept it; Connecticut organized it; Virginia, as we have seen, grasped it, and would not let it go; New York clung to it with vigor: and the struggle through which the Carolinas insisted on and secured it showed that it must be an organizing principle of the continent.

Nothing, indeed, can illustrate more brilliantly the difference between a theoretical legislation, however symmetrical its proportions, and that which has the vital spirit of a people in it and therefore is good for them because it fits them, than the reception given by the people of Carolina to the constitution drafted for them by Shaftesbury the statesman and Locke the philosopher. Viewed as a play of some of the best European notions of liberty into pure space, a leisurely exercise in political mathematics by reflective men immured in their libraries, it was no doubt a pleasant exercise to draw its outline; and if it had been applied to men without passions, a colony of human puppets, no doubt the machinery would have run without much friction. In the study of a philosophical lord what could be finer and more symmetrical than the division of Carolina into equal counties, with an Earl and two Barons for each, to whom a large portion of the land was forever deeded; the elective franchise conferred on freeholders of fifty acres; an aristocratic court to superintend the press: and a Parliament to which only large land-holders were eligible. But the social diagrams and the titles that looked so fine on English parchment could not be repeated in American fact. The soil would not support a Landgrave; the counties refused hospitality in their landscapes to a Baron's palace and estate: and the people found that they could not work at all in the artistic vestures of law which philosophy had cut and stitched for them. They resisted the blessing upon which so much philosophic ink and oil had been expended, and it was not many years before the model which, in England, as we read, "was esteemed by all judicious persons without compare," but under which the Carolinas had not known one day of real enjoyment, was forever abandoned, and the inhabitants trusted to their own wisdom and the organic power of their own sense of justice, as superior to all that scientific and foreign skill could accomplish in their behalf.

It was of great importance to the nobility and success of our revolution that there had been this steady, organizing force in the country from its earliest date. For it gave body to that struggle; it enabled the people to comprehend it from the first; it gave them something to grasp as an object for which to sacrifice, and to have a steady passion and a systematic enthusiasm for: and thus their devotion was saved from souring into a mad idea of popular discontent, suspicion, and ferocity, as all long contentions for embodied principles are sure at last to do. It is fortunate for us that it was not the rights of *man*, but the rights of *men*, that the Revolution affirmed and defended. In the felicitous language of the orator * whose admirable production adorned this occasion two years ago, 'the people fought for ideas that were facts and liberties that were laws.'

The next great step in the process of organization was through the blood, the storm, and the sacrifice of the Revolution, by which the colonies, achieving independence, rose to be *American States*. He who would know the glory of the struggle which this day commemorates, must study the quickening influence it exerted upon the republican principle in the land, so that it suddenly sprung into higher and vigorous forms. In most of the colonies, what-

---

* Edwin P. Whipple's Oration, p. 8, line 5.

ever aristocratic and feudal elements and prejudices lingered in the public mind, speedily disappeared during the progress of the struggle or at its close. The Tories were the scapegoats that bore away into banishment all the sentiment of that character that might lead the communities into public sin. The very statute books shook themselves free of all legislation that interfered with popular supremacy. It was not through violent disruptions and earthquake throes of society, but peacefully, that our Democracy · rose to its lasting empire. Even those whose interests were invaded by it offered no obstacles, when the revolution was over, to the full organizing sweep of the dominant idea. Its battle-grounds were conventions; its contests were speeches; its weapons were votes; its victories were laws: and public prosperity is the constant ovation it receives.

What a feature of our history is this, that all the experience and all the laws of society on the other continent have been contradicted and overridden in our growth; and while not a single privilege or right of the people in other countries has been gained at less expense than violent shocks and agitations, and the shedding of rivers of blood, here the germ of liberty · planted on a thin and frozen soil, has run through its upward stages without let or hinderance from ourselves, by the forth-putting power of its own life, revealing the gradual progress of its theory by some new shoot of institution or statute and showing in our history, through a process slightly less peaceful than the growing harvest, "first the blade, then the ear, after that the full corn in the ear." *Sans Culotte-ism*, as Carlyle describes it, came up into French society, like a fiend from the pit, snorting fire, and screaming to the terror-smitten nation "What will you do with me?" But from the ocean deeps of our history, through the blood-stained foam of the Revolution, rose the Republican Aphrodite, perfect in her proportions, blessing the day with a peaceful smile, whose presence the land she stepped upon rejoiced in, yielding the green herbs to her soft and delicate tread.

And now our attention must be given to the last and crowning stage of organization. The idea of a union among the colonies had floated through the popular mind, and it was gradually shaping itself into distinctness for years. There was the dim but deepening feeling, inspired by Providence, that the work of organization to which this continent was dedicated, would not be fulfilled till a central structure rose, that should represent the power and harmonize the interests of the lesser republics that were clustered on the soil. It was prophesied by the early union among the colonies of New England. Faint suggestions of the necessity of it were fostered by the growing oppressions of the parent land, making the colonies thrill with a common vexation and a common consciousness of wrong. A conception of it engaged the practical and patriotic brain of Franklin, and at one time was favorably viewed even in England. The peril of liberty in the years preceding the revolutionary outbreak acted as a consolidating pressure.

The general interests and passions, during the war, found a representative focus in the hall of the Continental Congress. In the confederation that succeeded, a stanch and legal bond was sought, for amity and power; but it was not wisely enough constructed to unify interests, and sectional passions and jealousies soon made ominous breaches in it. War was over; peace had come; but where was the one America that should have stood out shapely and strong, after the storm had blown away? The temple of western liberty was yet *unroofed*. The rock had been laid bare for its cornerstones; its foundations had been laid by a glorious company of workmen whose masonry needed no repair; its majestic columns had been raised in such stately strength, and with such various ornament, that the love of beauty and power in those who gazed upon them found little that was lacking; its peaceful enclosures were filled with thousands and hundreds of thousands whose fathers had laid the stubborn base and built the floors, and whose own genius and valor had lifted the pillars and carried up the walls.

But the covering of the vast edifice had baffled the skill of the architects. The Articles of Confederation were but an unsightly tent which the winds and the rain soon stripped into ribbons, leaving the multitudes unhoused under the fierce sunlight, the night skies, and the storm. Shall the constructive genius of the land prove unequal to this culminating problem? Has the victorious war imposed a duty which the conquerors cannot meet? Is the spectacle of shattered Germany and fragmentary Italy to be repeated in the unconstellated and hostile lights of the western firmament? and must the promise of our history and the pointings of Providence, and the hope of every preceding struggle, be fruitless, and the expectation of the world be denied its satisfaction? No, the intellect of the land is equal to the most difficult scheme of organization. For the great builders have gone aloft to consider the plans of a fitting superstructure. *He* is at their head whose sword bore no terror to the liberty which his military genius saved from foreign injury, and whose organizing character lifts the name of *Washington* higher than the fellowship of camps to the selectest list of statesmen. And now the mighty rafters of the Constitution rise, to be stretched from pillar to pillar across the walls; and see! the immense and glorious dome of the national government arches over the space below, to give shelter to the thronged and joyous multitudes, and from the staff that crowns it streams the banner of the One Republic, the last and greatest creation of a race in history.

Let it be our prayer that the dome thus raised may cover and crown the edifice for ages, that the flag which streams from its summit, stained though it is with many spots, shall float there, that the winds and the storms of public sentiment may wash it clean; knowing that the edifice is incomplete and weak without its coping and its roof, and that if the summit fall, it must be to the ruin of the walls and the burial of thousands by its crash.

Within our own generation the capacity of our country for the organization of liberty has made itself brilliantly manifest, and has won many triumphs. We have become so accustomed to the facts that we are not startled by the marvel which the facts reveal; but if we could look at it with fresh eyes and in the light of any other history than our own, we should see that our western colonization and the institutions that have kept pace with it, are so surprising that they might almost be accounted miraculous. When we see those mighty living tides of English, German, Irish, and Scandinavian emigration flowing westward and crystallizing as they flow into beautiful social order, where shall we turn to find anything in history by which it can be paralleled or even understood ? What is there in annals of time that will compare with the joyous song of humanity as it marches through the forests and valleys of the West, cutting the timber that obstructs its way into school-houses and churches, sweeping back the wolf and the deer, the buffalo and the bear, that instead of their howl and tramp, the air may be stirred with the eloquence of the caucus and the music of the choir, bidding the wild torrents and the fresh vapors hiss, and the implements of cunning labor fly, in compacting a civilization that combines freedom, culture, and religion, until the spirit that stepped upon the Plymouth sands is greeted by his grandchild at the Rocky Mountains and the free charter of California, — God save it from the disgrace of ever being other than free! — emblazons in the sight of China the principles caught from Faneuil Hall.

The human race has never, before this experience of the West, had the opportunity to show what results, in the way of organization, it could work if left alone.

One branch of the Christian Church in Europe throws its influence for the forces of despotism, on the ground that the human race itself is not equal to the production and maintenance of a new and beneficient institution. It affirms that the uninspired intellect of man is essentially anarchical, and that God has fixed by his own wisdom the forms of the family, the nobility, the throne, and the church, as the safeguards of all the peace that is possible; beyond which, if the irreverent ambition of man would stray, it ordains confusions and sins against Heaven. There is something sublime in the positive audacity of this theory, and humanity pleads against it with a rhetoric equally sublime. She brings deep latitudes and wide longitudes of liberty to answer it; she points to Cincinnati and Indianapolis, to a country between Lake Huron and Lake Michigan, to Wisconsin and Iowa, to the institutions that look down into the Pacific from the headlands of the Golden State and the Oregon, which have grown up without noise into order and prosperity, during the lifetime of the generations that have made Europe restless with throes for liberty, and while the logic has been promulgated which defames the popular power. Will it be said by the partisans of the theory in question that Providence has inspired the Americans for this work? Then Providence does not patronize despotism in the nineteenth century; and if our western countrymen have had no aid of inspiration, then the theory falls, for new institutions can grow out of, and rest upon, the popular mind.

On the continent of Europe, there is at this moment no political organization of men. They are agglomerated by force. They are heaped and crowded into tyrannical conditions, where their loves, reverences, and ideas will not suffer them to combine; government there bears the same relation to an organization that clay packed into a mould bears to a crystal.

The elements of modern civilization have always been jumbled there, and every effort which they have made of late for proper development and harmonious reconstruction has been met by lines of bayonets and blaze of cannon. It is well, therefore, that against the philosophy which supports the despots of the eastern world there should have arisen in our own day the magnificent refutation of the West; that the depths of our forests and the sweep of our prairies, should have answered the frown of St. Petersburg and the taunt of the Vatican, by a civilization whose rise is spotted with no drop of blood, and whose proportions show that the genius of our race, unhampered by despots, does know how to organize liberty in solid fact and vigorous law.

As we speak of the West, the subject itself, no less than our instinctive sympathy and sorrow, dictates an expression of respect and veneration for the memory of the statesman and the orator, whose worn frame, — the silent shrine of a rare, electric soul — will soon be laid for perpetual rest in that beloved soil. When his eyes first saw the light, the wilderness was scarcely broken, which, rapidly filling with hardy settlers, he helped in his early manhood to cover with American laws, and which, as a rising

State, he represented in the national councils, and glorified by his patriotism, his eloquence, his statesmanship, and a power of personal influence rarely equalled, and never, probably, surpassed.

> "From the charmed council to the festive board,
> Of human feelings the unbounded lord;
> In whose acclaim the loftiest voices vied,
> The praised — the proud — who made his praise their pride."

The business of eulogy is not for me or for this time. But the workings of American institutions can hardly find clearer and more brilliant illustration than in the fact that he, the great commoner, the Chatham of the Republic, was the child of poverty and the builder of his own greatness, rising early by the force of genius to a sway of men, more powerful than any titled autocrat can claim; and leaving such a vacancy as he sinks into his grave, that for thousands and hundreds of thousands in our land, the joy of this jubilee is dimmed by the thought that its dawning light and mid-day splendor fall upon the pale brow, the pulseless heart, the unnerved hand, and death-locked lips of HENRY CLAY.*

---

* Henry Clay was born in Hanover County, Va., 12 April, 1777, and died in Washington, D.C., 29 June, 1852.

Thus it has been the great distinction of our country that it has been the home of a more marvellous building capacity than any other land can show. Without having given to the world a single new work of much value to illumine the dark regions of social science, it has peopled a continent with institutions of which the projection in literature would have been denounced by lovers of order as a licentious and destructive dream. Nay, even for the best works that analyze and illustrate our own institutions, the American student is compelled to look abroad.

We are often stigmatized as a boasting people, too subject to gusts of extravagant impulses, too fond of exaggerated rhetoric, too much in love of showy and flattering words, and therefore at the mercy of the loose-tongued demagogue. We know on what aspects of society these charges are founded, but where is the people that in proportion to its talk has done so much that time will not attack ? But may we not claim it as a glorious distinction of our people, that though they are more than patient of florid rhetoric in the caucus and on the stump, they have always been distrustful of it in the Senate Chamber ? that they have always been wary of organizing declamation or flighty theory into a code? and that, so far as the attitude of the state towards new measures and other countries is concerned, it has been determined, not by whirlwinds of sentiment, but by cool reflection and sharp debates?

We may proudly hold it up as the peculiarity of our republic, that the people revere still the stiff speech of a statute more than they delight in frothy garrulities of fancy; and that before the plan of a demagogue can claim the sanction of those solemn words "be it enacted," it must pass through more refining processes than the heat of a caucus, and be hammered by some discussion that is solid with common sense. The men who hold the pens that write our statutes are generally organizers rather than dreamers and declaimers; and there is no more striking characteristic of our society than the fact that the gusty breath of a continental democracy has imparted so little instability and fluctuation to the laws.

The instructions which these thoughts furnish are simple and obvious. First, gratitude to the Providence that decreed this soil to men whose experiments for liberty were guided by a constructive instinct and a courageous prudence, rather than to men of more daring speculation and feebler hands. Who cannot see how much more has been done for liberty beyond our shores, by the slow and solid growth of *instituted* freedom here, than could have been done if the first million of inhabitants which our soil nourished, breaking up their homes, had returned to the Old World as crusaders against oppression? How fortunate that such myriads of Germans and Celts can come here and find not only the land welcoming them, but the homesteads and architecture of beneficent and tested institutions offering them protection! What if our past could be forgotten, and the millions of foreigners who press through our harbors toward the setting sun, were obliged to build their *liberties* as well as their log huts; to cultivate and organize the freedom they are to enjoy! How much less peace, how much less prosperity, would fall to their lot, than they now come in possession of, as inheritors of the principles and the consummate statesmanship of our Saxon builders in the past?

The mission of our land is still the path of organization, not aggressive propagandism or military interference. Let its influence be felt, in the lines of just and holy law, by process of construction through moral forces in favor of a higher national morality; by forcible protests against oppressive interference on the part of other nations in violation of the international code, but still with the dignity that shows the desire to keep the posture of peaceful friendship and practical instruction towards the European world.

Our responsibility to the oppressed of other lands is a deeper one than that of furnishing ammunition and supplies; it is the responsibility of faithfulness here to republican ideas, and of progress in the path suggested by the promptings of our history and the beckonings of Providence. Every noble institution we build up here is a more encouraging beacon to the struggling people of Europe than the fire-light of war. The striking off of each new fetter here resounds cheeringly through Europe. A musical tone travels much farther than a growl; and the effluence of a righteous victory of freedom on our shores will reach farther at last, and work more benefit for other races, than the sputter of our musketry in Trieste, and the roar of our floating batteries on the Danube. Let us not doubt that the wiping out of an oppressive statute in our code somehow makes the throne of Nicholas less firm. And all the prosperity, stability, and peace with which we invest the possession of freedom hasten the doom of foreign bondage, for they shed a light and a fragrance into the public sentiment that will guide the footsteps and revive the courage of the army of liberty in Europe, and they shame the lies that would brand republicanism as anarchy.

We have sent directly no ideas and no literature across the ocean to stir the popular heart to resistance, or to stimulate its aspirations; our influence has gone silently out from our institutions. The principle is as true with nations as in private life which Portia uttered, when she caught the gleam from home —

"How far that little candle throws its beams!
So shines a good deed in a naughty world."

Despotism entrenches itself behind our errors and sins almost as securely as behind its own artillery. Let us make our Union a cluster of Christian Commonwealths, and the death-knell of Absolutism is struck by the decree that makes *character* the highest force in civilization.

And so the second lesson of our theme warns us and beseeches us, as patriots and as lovers of the world, to go on in the work of organization. Our fathers have left us a work to do. We are no spiritual children of theirs if we believe that all which is desirable, and can be made safely operative in society, has been embodied here; and plainly enough there are unfinished portions of their scheme which it is for our generation and those who come after us, to complete, out of reverence for their memory, adoration of the truth and love of mankind.

If there is a race within our borders for which there is no organization of liberty, but upon whom the architecture of the Saxon institutions frowns like the sullen masonry of forts and jails; to whom their security is the security of the dungeon; and for whom the strength of law is the strength of bolts and chains: how plain is the call upon those of our people whose hands can help them, to consider their case in the light and by the methods of a practical and sinewy wisdom!

How plain is the call upon us to give up as miserable, vapid, and boyish, all the declamation which overlooks the rooted strength, and is weak enough to treat it as an *idea* which denunciation and rhetoric can expunge; and to take hold of it as a problem of life, that may take generations perhaps to solve, but yet that must be solved, guided by the fixed principle that there must come the time when every human being who stands on American soil shall have rights that are hedged by friendly statutes, and a sacred freedom which the whole spirit of society is pledged to maintain.

And in whatever way the spirit of social justice can be made to enter more deeply into our policy, or domesticate itself in new features of our code without disruption of order, — in plans of land reform, — in adjustments of the relations of labor, so that the laborer may be more efficiently a man, — in the projection of schemes for the safety and nurture of the perishing classes, — we are called on cautiously to make the experiment; and to show how far and with what results the *forces of society* may shoot out into regions that have hitherto been abandoned to grim laws of competition and caprices of private charity.

The grandeur and worth of our institutions call on us, as the inheritors of them, to remember the conditions, and inhale the spirit by which alone the most firmly founded organization can be upheld. It is a great thing that a body · has been given, so symmetrical and so vigorous, for the shrine of freedom here; that the organization of muscles and of nerves, of heart and brain, of limbs and bones, is so well balanced and so strong. But woe to us if we forget that every organism lives by inspiration, and by fresh breath, by regular activity and systematic food. We cannot maintain ourselves on the virtues of our fathers, nor support the frame of our freedom by glorying in their devotion, any more than our physical constitution can live on the food of last week, or the air we breathed upon the mountains last year. To support liberty there must be the wise love of it; the steady absorption, through the morality and faith of the people, of those juices and energies which are to every form of society what the soul is to its material abode.

Or if we are insensible to fear for the downfall of our institutions, still let us remember that no nation can rely on the past for its attitude, its expression, and its character. A man inherits his physical frame; but though it be symmetrical as that of Apollo, or muscular as that of Hercules, it depends on his own spirit, his virtues or his vices, whether his countenance shall be charming or ugly, whether nobility or vulgarity shall stream from his features, and his influence be a help or a hinderance to the laws of good. And so a nation, though it have the most fitly woven texture of institutions for its body, must from its own ideal resources pervade them with a soul; and its beauty and nobleness will be judged by mankind according to the expression with which it beams, the selfishness or the charity, the brutal force or the generous chivalry, which it represents by its *countenance* among the brotherhood of states.

Let us turn the instruction which our history furnishes, to trust in the capacity of the people for organization to another quarter; let us make it general and generous. Dispiriting estimates have become quite too common among us of the ability of the nations on the continent of Europe to take care of themselves. Alas! if Americans are to swell the chorus which despots have led, that the best bulwarks of order in Italy, Germany, Hungary, and France are cannon and court-martials; that it is better to have the order of bayonets and the iron discipline of the camp, than to let the popular genius effervesce until it settles into wisdom; and if it is to go forth that we have more sympathy with the tramp of the Russian legions, as they tread out the flaming Magyar principles into the blood of the hearts that fed them, than we have in

Kossuth's power to establish there the institutions which the people love. Alas! if because France has been cursed with a few mental fiends, who would build up a *red republic*, we are to look with complacency on the gambling tyranny that dictates a despotic constitution from the mouth of perjury, that steals by <u>one trick</u> of universal suffrage the chance to crush the right of representation and choke the press, that distributes the functions of government among epaulettes, and that graciously grants to the nations the right and the blessing of unrestricted trade.

Where is the American spirit that should be nurtured by our institutions, if, in the very light of our history, we are to distrust the power of the people to organize better institutions for themselves than the brain of a tyrant can devise? Do you say that the path of revolution for Europe is a perilous and shaded way? We know it. But the last spirit to be fostered in the American breast is that which would bring all the perils that may beset the popular effort for self-government into any comparison with the quiet maintained by unscrupulous despotism. Institutions like ours Europe may not be able to establish, may not devise, may not desire; a long and bloody storm may intervene between the overthrow of oppression and the organization of peace; but it is not for us to preach and nourish hopeless distrust of the ability of popular Europe, — if left for a generation, or for half a century, in the experiment of liberty, — to correct mistakes, to prune excesses, and to find the preparation for republicanism which we so earnestly talk about, but which will never be gained by living under the shadow of absolute thrones.

And finally, we are warned by our history not to distrust the capacity of the human race to attain a social order upon the earth of a higher stamp than any yet secured. It is *justice* which, thus far in human experience, has been heaving the foundations of society, that some of its principles may gain a solid place. The great struggle has been to balance the interests of the masses against the power of the few, so that nature might be, in some sense, a home for them, and existence a blessing. In the institution of such justice, at least for the white races, our land stands preëminent, far ahead of the nations that have gone before. Two centuries ago it would have seemed impossible, Utopian, to the wisest statesman and thinkers of the other world, to realize on a scale such as this country now exhibits, such a scheme of self-supporting, orderly and stable democracy. But there are dreams of men, yes, promises of a wisdom higher than man's, that this earth is yet to be the scene of organizations nobler than those of justice, — organizations of *love*. It is inspiring to think of some far-off centuries as destined to witness the birth, the progress, and the completion of such a blessing for our race. And, looking at our condition from the cruel feudal times, or from the level of a Patagonian degradation, such an organization of love upon the earth does not seem wholly a dream. And so this great value belongs to our history, that the philosophy of it helps our Christian hope. It makes prophecy seem more sober. It brings the rhetoric of Isaiah within the sympathy of common sense.

It is a summit from which the thinker may look off, like Moses from the mount, upon new and charming fields lying sweet in the smile of Heaven, where the armies of humanity — that have come up out of the bondage of despotism, and marched with sadness, but with courage, through the wastes and the want of the desert of selfishness, — shall find a home, shall build amid plenty, and enjoy in peace; and the nations, bound into solidarity of life despite their varieties, — as the globe, with all its latitudes and zones, its polar and tropic climes, its mountains and prairies, its streams and seas, is organized into one physical republic, — "shall beat their swords into ploughshares and their spears into pruning-hooks," and praise the Creator through a life of song, labor, and prayer.

www.ingramcontent.com/pod-product-compliance
Lightning Source LLC
Chambersburg PA
CBHW031503040426
42444CB00007B/1186